Do You Wonder WHY?

How to Answer Life's Tough Questions

Do You Wonder WHY?

How to Answer Life's Tough Questions

by David Pouilloux
Illustrated by François Cointe
Edited by Kate O'Dare

sunscreen

Library of Congress Cataloging-in-Publication Data

Pouilloux, David.
Do you wonder why? : how to answer life's tough questions /
by David Pouilloux; illustrated by Francois Cointe; English translation
by Willard Wood.
p. cm.
Includes bibliographical references and index.
ISBN 978-1-4197-0389-8 (alk. paper)
1. Identity (Psychology) 2. Self-esteem in adolescence. 3. Parent and child.
4. Interpersonal relations. I. Title.
BF697.P6948 2012
646.70083—dc23
2012016673

Printed and bound in China
10 9 8 7 6 5 4 3 2 1

Amulet Books are available at special discounts when purchased in quantity
for premiums and promotions as well as fund-raising or educational use.
Special editions can also be created to specification. For details, contact
specialsales@abramsbooks.com or the address below.

ABRAMS
THE ART OF BOOKS SINCE 1949
115 West 18th Street
New York, NY 10011
www.abramsbooks.com

contents

Peers   Why do people smoke and drink even though it's

bad for them?

Why do people always want to be right (even when

they're wrong)?

Why did my friend betray me?

Why do people make fun of others?

Love   Why doesn't my crush want to go out with me?

Why do I worry about getting dumped?

Why did I go out with that person even though I

didn't really like him or her?

Why am I afraid to be a bad kisser?

Why does that person flirt with me but not want to

go out with me?

Why don't I ever fall in love?

Why don't I want a boyfriend or girlfriend?

Why do boys think about sex all the time?

Why do I flirt with everybody?

Conclusion

WHY, WHY, WHY,

WHY, WHY, WHY,

WHY, WHY, WHY,

WHY, WHY, WHY,

WHY, WHY, WHY,

WHY, WHY, WHY,

WHY, WHY, WHY,

WHY, WHY, WHY,

Life is filled with questions. And sometimes it's hard to get good answers to them. Maybe you want to ask your parents something, but you feel embarrassed. Or maybe you ask a friend, and he or she doesn't know the answer. You might be left with no idea where to turn.

That's where this book comes in: It addresses some of the biggest, strangest, and most important questions floating around in your head, to help you make sense of what you're feeling and what's going on in your life. This book is organized into sections of questions and answers about the things you worry about most: yourself, your parents, your peers, and love. When you have questions, Sunscreen has the answers!

who am i?

why don't i know
who i really am?

The truth is, a lot of people ask themselves this same question, and it's OK if you're not sure what the answer is just yet.

It's a tough question to answer because there are a lot of different qualities that make you who you are: your appearance, your opinions, your

knowledge, your goals, etc. And these qualities change all the time as you grow and learn and experience new things. You also have to deal with a lot of different influences in your life. From your family and friends to movies and books, there's always new and different information coming your way!

It can be overwhelming to make sense of all these things, and it will take time to put together all the pieces of the puzzle that make up your personality. The answer to "Who am I?" is constantly changing, and it's tough to make sense of a "me" that's continually in motion. The thing is, you'll always experience new ideas, new people, and new projects that create a new sense of *you* every day. Feeling that things are always changing can be scary, but it also means that you can ultimately be whoever you want to be!

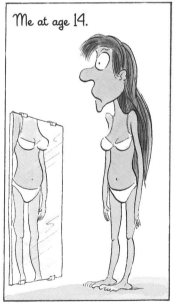

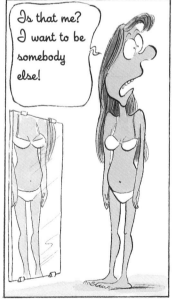

why do some people say
i have no style?

Some people think that having "style" means following the latest trends: buying certain clothes, wearing their hair a certain way, etc., based on what they see in the media or have been told is cool. But style is really about expressing yourself, and that means wearing what makes *you* feel good, not others. Besides, what's the fun in wearing what everyone else is wearing?

If you find yourself being criticized for your personal style, try not to let it bother you. Some people will always judge others who don't follow trends or who like different things than they do. However, if the advice is friendly and sincere, it could be worthwhile to be open-minded. If you're unsure, asking someone you trust for an opinion could be helpful. Personal styles evolve and change and it's fun to give many looks a try. Your style can be whatever you make it. You might like to wear camouflage one day and floral patterns the next. As long as you dress in a way that makes you feel comfortable, that's all that matters! Have fun with your style and express the inner you.

why do i feel
scared of things?

Suddenly, he heard it: Something was moving toward him in the pitch-black forest. Chad was filled with terror. What was it? The shrubs in front of him began to shake, and a bloodcurdling howl filled his ears. The monster leapt forward, its razor-sharp claws bared. It shrieked again, and poor Chad was paralyzed, sitting in his seat at the movie theater.

It's normal to be frightened of scary movies—they're supposed to be scary! And it can be fun to feel scared when you want to feel that way. But there may be things that scare you or make you nervous in your daily life, like spiders or heights. Those are things you don't have control over, which can make some people uncomfortable or afraid. Maybe there are other things that you're scared of because you don't feel confident in yourself. For example, maybe you're afraid to speak up in class. It's not the talking part that's scary—it's people's reactions you're concerned about. You might worry that your classmates won't listen to you or that they'll make fun of you. If you have a fear like this—a fear that other people will think you're not good enough in some way—remember that what's most important is having confidence! Sometimes, you also just need to try new things—anything can be scary the first time, but after some practice, new tasks or situations get easier. When you give new things a try, the things that scared you before won't seem so scary anymore.

why do i feel
so ugly?

At this time in your life, you're going through a lot of physical changes, and you haven't fully developed yet. This can make you feel insecure about your appearance, and maybe you're not sure what to do to feel better. Maybe right now you're depending on other people to tell you that you're beautiful. You may think that if people tell you you're pretty or ugly, it must be true. But the truth is that everyone has different ideas of what makes someone attractive, so you shouldn't take any one person's opinion to heart.

You might also be comparing yourself to people you see in movies and on TV. Everywhere you look, you see images—almost always digitally enhanced—of perfect faces and bodies. Spending time comparing yourself to them or to the most beautiful people at school might increase your own feelings of ugliness.

How do you get through all of this? Do your best to listen to compliments and ignore teasing. Thinking that you're ugly can prevent you from highlighting the things about yourself that are beautiful or handsome or special. When you feel good in your own skin, you are much more likely to look in the mirror and see the good things.

And remember, even Angelina Jolie and Selena Gomez have bad hair days! Everyone feels insecure about his or her looks. The key is trying to be positive and confident and remembering you're not alone.

why does everybody
call me a nerd?

Being smart and getting good grades is something to be proud of. But it doesn't always feel that way if people make fun of you for it. The truth is, people who make fun of you for being a "nerd" are probably jealous of your success. They most likely feel insecure and are acting out in a way to make themselves feel better, even if that means making you feel bad.

You should take pride in your intelligence and your work in school, but you should also remember that things that come easily to you might not come as easily to others. Maybe algebra is a piece of cake for you, but some of your friends are struggling with it. It might hurt their feelings if you talk about how easy you thought a test was. If they feel comfortable enough to bring up their struggles with you, perhaps you could offer to help. And if you're with people who you know aren't as interested in school as you are, finding other things to talk about that you're both interested in will help to avoid tension. What's most important is that you enjoy learning and school, not what other people have to say about it.

why do i prefer to be
by myself?

You might know people who couldn't survive if they didn't have tons of friends around all the time. Being by themselves is the last thing they want. But maybe you're the kind of person who does like being alone and having time to do your own thing, whether that's reading, playing games, or even just thinking.

If being alone sometimes is a choice that makes you happy, that's OK! There's no rule that says you need to share everything in your life with two, three, or fifty people to be happy. You can prefer having time to draw, work on your computer, write, play music, or even take a walk by yourself.

It's all about balance. Sometimes you want to be alone, but sometimes it's worth your while to start a conversation or work or play with others, even if they are very different from you. Showing interest in what other people are doing and asking a few questions are good ways to reach out. It's OK to spend time by yourself, as long as you don't close yourself off completely from other people.

why am i afraid of not being
like everyone else?

It's normal to want to fit in and be part of a group. But it can be difficult when the things you like and the things everyone else seems to like are different. It can be tempting to stop saying what you think and just go along with what everybody else is saying. You might be worried that if you say what's really on your mind, then people will laugh at you, or you might end up agreeing with others to avoid conflict. But if you follow along instead of thinking for yourself, you risk missing out on what *you* really want. You could end up wearing clothes you don't like, listening to music that bores you, and just not enjoying yourself. In the end, this fear of not fitting in can stifle your personality.

Being yourself often requires some courage. You have to accept that people will disagree with you sometimes. They might even feel threatened by your independence and try to get you to back down. Maybe you get teased, and that teasing makes you doubt yourself. That can be difficult to deal with, but it's important to do the things that make you happy, even if those things aren't what other people are doing. Besides, being unique is way cooler than being just like everyone else!

why don't i know what i want to do
in the future?

It's normal to be unsure of what you want to do in the future. One day you may want to be a chef, and the next you might want to be a lawyer. At this point in your life, your interests are still changing, and it will take some time to figure out what you're most passionate about and what you want to pursue as a career.

As you learn about the world and all the different careers and ways of life

open to you, it makes sense that you won't immediately have a clear vision of what you want to do. And once you do make a decision, you may end up changing your mind!

But you might feel that there's pressure on you to figure it out now. Maybe your family or teachers have started asking you about it. You know they care, and you'd like to give them an answer, but you're just not sure what that answer is yet. It's OK to be honest and say you're unsure.

For now, focus on the subjects and activities that interest you most. If you find something that really appeals to you, you could do some research about it and see if there are any related careers that you think you might like. Eventually, you'll figure out what you really want to do.

Right now my books are helping me get to the remote Dad hid on top of the bookshelf. But once I'm grown up, what good are they going to do me?

why do i have to learn
all this boring stuff?

In school, you're learning about a lot of things: ancient history, genetics, the Pythagorean theorem, and more. Among all your subjects and classes, there are going to be some that feel more—or less—useful to you. You can't imagine how some of them will possibly come in handy later on, either in your everyday life or in your career. For some people, math is the greatest thing ever, and they can't understand why they have to read so many books in English class. For others, it's just the opposite. Since everyone has different strengths and weaknesses, taking a variety of subjects gives everybody the chance to try different things and experiment with what interests them most.

Learning about many things also gives you more well-rounded knowledge, and learning about something in a subject you're not crazy about may end up helping you in a subject that you *are* crazy about. Maybe you learn something in history class that has to do with the book that you're reading for English class, or maybe you learn a formula in math that helps you understand something you're learning about in science. Whatever the case, learning about a lot of different things will help increase your overall knowledge. And you never know when something that seems boring will actually turn out to be really cool!

why is reading so
boring for me?

If you don't enjoy reading, that could mean that you're reading the wrong stuff. It can be exciting to find a book that you just can't put down, and that kind of a book is easier to find than you might think!

Reading can allow you to live vicariously, or through the experiences of somebody else. You can be in a world with witches flying on broomsticks, or talking cats, or vampires, even though you're just sitting with a book on a school bus.

Thanks for the present, Mom—but the touch screen doesn't work.

But maybe fiction and fantasy don't interest you. You don't feel connected to what you're reading about because you don't feel like you can relate. Maybe you'd rather read about facts and ideas instead of stories. There are books like that out there, too! There are lots of nonfiction books that discuss interesting facts, whether they're about history, science, math, or any other topic.

The key to enjoying reading is to figure out what it is you like in a book. Whether it's fantasy, adventure, nonfiction, or another genre, when you read something that hooks you, it's a great feeling. The books that can make you feel this way already exist, and when you find them, you won't be able to put them down!

parents

why do my parents fight even though they say they love each other?

Love is not always simple or predictable. In the midst of hugs, good conversations, and fun, there can be moments when suddenly your parents are angry with each other. Maybe your mom is annoyed, and your dad's feelings are hurt. Whatever the case, it's important to remember that it's normal for people who love each other to fight sometimes.

People who love each other do not necessarily agree about everything. Sometimes even little disagreements can spark a fight: what to put in a salad, how to cook a chicken, or even what you should or shouldn't be allowed to do. A fight can mark the beginning of a discussion in which your parents will share their opinions and try to come to an agreement on what works best for both of them. At first, the exchange may be tense, but then things may calm down again. It's a recurring part of a couple's life: They love each other, but they constantly have to come to an agreement about a ton of things.

Another possibility is that things are tense between your parents simply because they're tired or stressed out. This isn't necessarily something to worry about: They love each other—they're just exhausted and cranky from all the things they need to do every day.

Fights happen, but once you move on from them, what's most important is to be able to discuss the situation without being hurtful. Continuing an argument may do more harm than good, so it's important to know how to explain yourself, how to recognize mistakes, how to reach out to the other person and say you're sorry. Often you won't be able to remember what started the whole thing in the first place, or it will seem unimportant.

why do my parents want me to go to bed
so early?

Having to go to bed at nine p.m. feels like a huge waste of time. Yes, you understand that you need sleep to be alert for school, and, yes, your body needs to rest. And you know that all those neurons in your brain have been busy all day and need some downtime. But you still don't want to go to bed! You want to be up and doing things.

Think about how you feel the day after you stay up really late and only get a few hours of sleep. You probably feel very tired, and it's harder to do things and enjoy your day. If your parents are telling you to go to bed early, it's because they want you to be able to function the next day. If you're really not tired, you can always try to compromise with them: Asking for another half hour might not seem unreasonable if there's something you want to finish up before bed. And even if you go to your room to get ready for bed, you don't have to go to sleep right away. You can read, write in your journal, do some thinking, or other quiet activities!

why do my parents bug me about watching too much TV or being on the computer too much?

𝒰𝓈𝒾𝓃𝑔 𝓉𝒽𝑒 𝒸𝑜𝓂𝓅𝓊𝓉𝑒𝓇 𝑜𝓇 𝓌𝒶𝓉𝒸𝒽𝒾𝓃𝑔 𝒯𝒱 can be a lot of fun. Maybe you have some favorite TV shows you like to watch or some blogs you like to read. While that's all OK, what probably worries your parents is if you start to spend too much time watching TV or being on the computer. They want you to be active and do more than just sit in front of a screen.

Sometimes that might seem unfair, but it's important to find a balance. For example, when it's a beautiful day outside, going for a swim in the pool in your backyard instead of playing another online game might be a nice change of pace. Being physically active is important to staying healthy, and engaging in a variety of activities can keep your mind in good shape, too!

Also, playing an online game doesn't involve the same sort of interaction as playing volleyball or basketball. Although you can play video games with other kids, face-to-face interaction and teamwork are a different kind of fun and use other skills. These kinds of games can be satisfying in a way that playing a computer game or watching TV can't.

why won't my parents let me do things
other kids can do?

Rules vary from family to family. When you hang out with friends, you might feel that their parents let them do whatever they want and give them way more freedom. You might think that your parents treat you unfairly, and you don't understand why they don't let you do more.

No two parenting styles are the same. For example, some parents may want their kids to act independently, while other parents are very protective. Some may think it's important for their children to play sports, while others think music is more important. Basically, what works for your friends' parents might not work for yours.

It can be tough when you want to do something and your parents won't let you. Sometimes it can help to try to see the situation from their perspective so that you can address their concerns. For example, it makes sense that your parents might be worried about letting you go to the house of someone they've never met before. They don't know this person or his or her parents, so they don't know for sure that you'll be in a good environment. If that's the case, maybe you could invite the person over to your house instead. Having him or her over can allow your parents to meet this new person and feel more comfortable. Reaching a compromise can often be a good solution.

It's also important to show your parents that you're responsible and that they can trust you. So when they tell you to call them from the party when you get there, you should follow through. When they ask you to be home from Andy's house at eight, be on time. The more you behave responsibly, the more freedom you'll have.

why do my parents embarrass me
sometimes?

There might be times when you feel embarrassed by your parents. Maybe your dad makes a really bad joke, or you don't like the clothes your mom wears. Maybe you feel bad that your parents embarrass you, but you can't help it. The truth is, it's a normal thing that happens to most kids. As you grow up, your critical senses develop and you begin to make judgments, even about your parents.

When you were younger, you might have thought that your parents were perfect and that everything they did was great. But now you're realizing that they're just regular people, with good and bad qualities like anybody else. Your perspective has changed, and now you might consider some of their traits to be bad in some way.

The key to not feeling embarrassed is to shift your perspective and learn to accept the people you love as just that: people. By smiling and laughing at those faults that bother you (rather than grimacing and groaning), you may even be able to appreciate the things that make your parents who they are. And keep in mind that your parents are no worse than any others. Ask your friends about their embarrassing parents, and you might just get an earful!

peers

why do people smoke and drink even though
it's bad for them?

It's no secret that smoking cigarettes and drinking alcohol can be damaging to you. But some people still do it anyway. People start for different reasons: Some might do it to try to fit in, while others might do it to make them feel more adult. Holding a cigarette or a drink can also feel like a little shield for some people. They feel less awkward and more at ease.

People often tell themselves that they'll be able to break the habit, but smoking cigarettes and abusing alcohol are tough habits to break. Because we see people drinking and smoking all the time, it might not seem like such a big deal. But both substances are drugs, and they can create dependency and addiction. That means that once you get used to using them, it gets harder and harder to stop. And, despite the risks, you need to use them more and more just to feel normal.

The easiest way to avoid this is to never start at all. That way you know you won't get addicted. You have the right to say no when your friends ask you if you want to drink or smoke. You may not want to say no to your friends, and maybe you want to live in the moment and have new experiences and try different things. But the choices you make today will have effects on your health tomorrow.

why do people always
want to be right
(even when they're wrong)?

It's often hard for people to admit when they're wrong. When you're right, you may feel more important and even powerful. You've shown that you are knowledgeable, and people may come to you with questions. It's nice to be respected and trusted in this way, and it boosts your confidence. Everyone from your parents to your teachers and friends experiences these feelings too.

While it's understandable to want to be "in the know," it's important not to take that too far. For instance, if people start lying just so others will think they're right, it can cause a lot of problems. There may be arguments and hurt feelings, and people could even get into fights. It's just not worth it.

It can be really hard to talk to someone who insists on being right. He or she contradicts what you say, and it's hard for you to express yourself when someone else is telling you that you're wrong.

The best thing people can do is try to listen to other viewpoints and be open-minded. Allowing oneself to consider new ideas can be an eye-opening and even fun experience. And when you exchange ideas with others, you might come up with even better ideas!

why did my friend
betray me?

When you tell a friend a secret, you trust him or her to keep it. But sometimes secrets are shared when they shouldn't be, and that can be upsetting. You may feel betrayed and angry. You thought you could tell your friend anything, but now you don't trust him or her. You may even wonder if you want to be friends with that person anymore.

The truth is, a friendship isn't always perfect. Things can go wrong, and feelings can get hurt. When something like that happens, it's important

to really think about the situation and try not to overreact. Give the other person a chance to apologize and explain what happened from his or her perspective. Maybe it was all a big misunderstanding and you can work things out. Or maybe it's not a misunderstanding and you realize that the person isn't the good friend you thought he or she was. Either way, it's important to listen to the other person and find out his or her side of the story.

why do people
make fun of others?

It's hurtful to be made fun of, and it's hard to understand why someone would want to make another person feel bad. There are a lot of different reasons that people make fun of others. It could be that they feel uncomfortable with all the changes they're going through—physically, mentally, emotionally—and they really don't like themselves very much. Turning the attention to someone else seems like a great idea. But eventually people might not want to be around those people anymore because the meanness is too much to take. It's difficult to remain friends with someone who is always so negative and insecure. The truth is, you'll make more friends—and keep them—by being nice.

love

why doesn't my crush want to
go out with me?

Crushing on someone? Even though it's normal, that doesn't mean it's easy, especially if the other person doesn't feel the same. You may wonder why and start to doubt yourself: "Am I ugly? Am I a loser? What do I need to change?"

But the problem isn't you. Unfortunately, love isn't simple, and sometimes the person you think is right for you really isn't. And a new haircut or outfit won't change your crush's mind. (If it does, then he or she doesn't like you for the right reasons anyway!)

Being rejected feels terrible, but it doesn't mean that you aren't wonderful or that you won't find love. If you've never had a boyfriend or girlfriend before, that's because you haven't met the right person yet. Don't give up!

why do i worry about
getting dumped?

Getting rejected is not a fun thing to go through. And if you really like

someone, it's hard not to worry whether that person feels as strongly about

you. You may be afraid that they'll lose interest or get bored with you. When

someone breaks up with you, you may feel hurt and even embarrassed.

But when it doesn't work out with someone, try to remember that the

person was just not the right fit for you. Maybe you didn't have as much in

common as you thought you did, or maybe he or she turned out to be different in some way.

If you get dumped, it isn't because you're a loser, or uptight, or don't know how to kiss. Everybody is looking for different things in a relationship, and when you find someone who wants the same things you do, you won't have to worry about getting dumped.

why did i go out with that person even though i didn't really like him or her?

Deciding whether or not to go out with someone isn't always easy. Sometimes you might feel lonely and want the attention. Sometimes you may not be sure how you feel about the person and decide to give him or her a chance, only to find out that he or she wasn't right for you. Whatever the situation, romantic feelings aren't always simple.

Going out with somebody who is funny, kind, and respectful, even if you don't have the world's most powerful feelings for him or her, isn't a bad thing! Anyone who tells you they've only dated people they were madly in love with is lying. Only in fairy tales do people go around falling magically in love at first sight. It's no surprise that you may find yourself agreeing to go out with someone even if your feelings for him or her aren't overwhelming. You want attention and affection. And you never know for sure how you'll feel about someone until you actually give him or her a chance. Feelings can change when you least expect it!

why am i afraid to be a
bad kisser?

At least once in our lives, we all confront a terrible fear: What if we kiss someone and it is a totally horrible, absolutely atrocious, monumentally bad kiss? The thought of messing up a kiss, especially your first one, can be a major source of anxiety. Why? For a lot of reasons: You're afraid of doing it wrong, drooling too much, biting the other person by mistake, having bad breath, etc. And you worry that you won't measure up to other people the person has kissed.

We all want the first kiss to be incredible and perfect, but that's a lot of pressure. That's why the most important thing you can do is relax. Remind

Practicing kissing with girls I meet online is maybe not the best idea . . .

yourself that it's OK if things don't go perfectly. A love story can still happen even if it starts with a pretty bad kiss. Kissing can be like getting to know somebody; it takes a while to break the ice and start enjoying the conversation.

There's no secret recipe for being an amazing kisser. Not everybody likes the same thing. You can ace a kiss with one person and fail miserably with the next, even though you did the exact same thing. You are free to kiss in whatever way you want, and if you kiss badly once in a while, you can make up for it the next time.

why does that person flirt with me but not want to
go out with me?

Sometimes it's hard to know exactly what another person is feeling. Someone might send you signals like smiles, winks, and hugs, but just when it seems serious, he or she is no longer interested. "What? Go out with you? Me? Never!"

People don't always know what they want, and sometimes people just like to feel liked. They enjoy the attention they're getting and will continue to do the things that get them that attention—even if it means flirting with someone they're not really interested in.

There's nothing wrong with flirting—as long as you don't take advantage of someone else's feelings.

Watch out for Aphrodite over there. She'll light your fire but let you burn.

why don't i ever
fall in love?

Love can be unpredictable, and you never know when it might come your way! It can be hard to wait, especially when you see other people who are happy and in love. But love takes time and requires patience.

Real love isn't always love at first sight. It might take time to find the right person and for love to develop. And there's no secret formula to making love happen; it's different for everyone. The most important thing you can do is be yourself and be open to other people.

Love won't just pass you by!

why don't i want a boyfriend
or girlfriend?

Having a boyfriend or girlfriend can be great, but it can also be a little stressful. You may worry about what your significant other thinks of you, so you try to act in a certain way around him or her. Or maybe you get nervous and don't always know what to talk about. You also might feel unsure about things like kissing or holding hands in public because you're worried about what people will say.

With friends, things are usually simpler. You can act goofy with your friends and not worry that they'll get the wrong idea about you. You can easily spend the day with them and not feel nervous or bored. Boyfriends and girlfriends can be more complicated.

Whether you don't feel ready to have a boyfriend or girlfriend or you just don't want to deal with the stress of it right now, that's OK! You probably won't feel like this forever. Everyone develops feelings at his or her own rate, and there's no rush. Maybe you'll meet someone special and change your mind. Until then, there's nothing wrong with doing your own thing.

why do boys think about sex
all the time?

The truth is, boys don't necessarily think of sex more often than girls do. Just like girls, boys think about lots of things besides sex: friends, games, sports, music, families, vacation, questions about the future, etc. But sometimes they express their thoughts about sex differently. Maybe they tell jokes or tease one another. They may want to show off to impress their friends, and they think that cracking crude jokes will somehow make them seem cool.

But there's no harm in thinking about sex. Whether you're a boy or a girl, it's normal to wonder about your sexuality. During adolescence, your hormones are starting to change your body and mind, and you are beginning to experience desire. This can cause a lot of different changes, including increased thoughts about sex. But at this point, sexuality is still a little scary and mysterious.

Some boys might be eager to pretend that isn't the case for them—of course they know everything already! Making jokes and bragging is a way of dealing with their anxieties, doubts, and fears.

why do i
flirt with everybody?

𝓕𝓵𝓲𝓻𝓽𝓲𝓷𝓰 𝔀𝓲𝓽𝓱 𝓹𝓮𝓸𝓹𝓵𝓮 𝓬𝓪𝓷 𝓫𝓮 𝓯𝓾𝓷. The smiles or second glances you get might make you feel special and important. You also might feel as if flirting puts you in control, and that can be a nice feeling.

But it can also be easy to go a little overboard with flirting. If you're always flirting—saying things and acting in certain ways to gain attention—then people might have a hard time getting to know the real you. And the only way to have a true connection with someone is to be yourself. The best thing to do is remember that you don't have to be the charmer all the time. When you act natural, chances are that people will still be drawn to you, and, even better, they'll like you for who you are.

conclusion

Now that you've read this book, we hope some of your tough questions have been answered! When you're not sure about something, you can flip back through these pages for help. A trusted adult or friend is always a good resource as well. Remember that all teens are going through the same changes and struggling with the same concerns. Life is full of questions, and part of growing up is questioning who you are, as well as the world around you. Never stop asking why. Be confident and stay true to yourself—and you will find the answers.

index

suggestions for further reading

The Kids' Book of Questions
Gregory Stock, PhD
New York: Workman Publishing, 2004.

American Medical Association Boy's Guide to Becoming a Teen
Amy B. Middleman, MD, MSEd, MPH, and Kate Gruenwald Pfeifer, LCSW
San Francisco: Jossey-Bass, 2006.

American Medical Association Girl's Guide to Becoming a Teen
Amy B. Middleman, MD, MSEd, MPH, and Kate Gruenwald Pfeifer, LCSW
San Francisco: Jossey-Bass, 2006.

YOU: The Owner's Manual for Teens: A Guide to a Healthy Body and Happy Life
Michael F. Roizen, MD, Mehmet C. Oz, MD, and Ellen Rome, MD, MPH
New York: Free Press, 2007.

The 6 Most Important Decisions You'll Ever Make: A Guide for Teens
Sean Covey
New York: Fireside, 2006.